AI Crafting Precision

The Art of Effective Queries
in AI Conversations

by Bruce Goldwell

DO YOU SUPPORT VETERANS?

Your _feedback_ (REVIEW) is invaluable in improving my authorship.

As a proud Vietnam Veteran, I dedicate my life to supporting fellow Veterans in need.

I humbly ask for your assistance.

You can make a difference in the lives of vets as well as my own by simply "**_reading and reviewing_**" my books, before sharing them with your family and friends.

With your help, I can expand the reach of my novels and grow my community of readers. As the fan base strengthens, so will my book royalties, **_allowing me to not only channel financial aid towards homeless veterans_**, but also extend support to anyone facing life's challenges.

"Your Review holds immense power";

together, we can change lives.

Visit www.imalocalauthor.com for info on my books.

Bruce Goldwell

Table of Contents

AI Crafting Precision

The Art of Effective Queries
in AI Conversations

"Wisdom isn't knowing everything-

it's knowing when to learn from others."

Precision Unleashed

The Art and Science of Crafting Laser-Sharp Requests for AI Interaction

The effectiveness of interacting with ChatGPT relies heavily on the specificity and detail of the user's requests. The more precisely users communicate their needs, the more context and guidance ChatGPT receives, resulting in responses that are better tailored to their requirements. This concept is rooted in the nature of how language models like ChatGPT generate responses based on input patterns and context.

When users provide specific and detailed requests, they provide ChatGPT with a clearer understanding of their expectations, enabling the model to produce more accurate, relevant, and nuanced responses. This is particularly crucial in scenarios where users seek specific information, creative content, or expert-level insights. Let's break down the key aspects of why specificity matters in interacting with ChatGPT:

1. Contextual Understanding:

 - Specific requests offer ChatGPT a more comprehensive understanding of the user's intent. For example, asking, "Can you explain the impact of climate change on biodiversity in rainforests?" provides a clearer context compared to a generic request like, "Tell me about climate change."

2. Relevance and Precision:

 - Specificity ensures that the generated responses are directly relevant to the user's needs. For instance, requesting, "Provide detailed examples of how artificial intelligence is transforming the healthcare industry" yields a more precise answer compared to a broader request like, "Tell me about AI."

3. Complex Problem Solving:

 - When users present complex scenarios or problems with detailed parameters, ChatGPT can engage in more elaborate problem-solving. For instance, asking, "Given a hypothetical scenario of an economic recession, how might investment strategies differ for various industries?" allows for a more nuanced exploration compared to a vague inquiry like, "Economic recession."

4. Creative Content Generation:

- In creative tasks, such as storytelling or idea generation, specificity guides ChatGPT in tailoring content to the user's preferences. For example, requesting, "Craft a science fiction story set on a distant exoplanet with sentient plant life and explorers facing an environmental crisis" offers a more personalized narrative compared to a generic prompt like, "Write me a story."

5. Expert-Level Insights:

- In specialized domains, detailed requests help ChatGPT provide expert-level insights. For instance, asking, "Analyze the impact of blockchain technology on supply chain management, considering both advantages and challenges" enables a more in-depth exploration compared to a broad question like, "Tell me about blockchain."

6. Efficient Communication:

   - Specific requests facilitate efficient communication, saving time and iterations. Users can receive the information or content they need more promptly when their queries are clear and detailed.

7. Personalization:

   - Specificity allows for a more personalized experience. When users provide details about their preferences, such as tone, style, or specific requirements, ChatGPT can tailor responses to align with those preferences.

In summary, the principle is simple: the more specific and detailed the request, the more ChatGPT can comprehend and address the user's needs accurately. This concept underscores the collaborative nature of interactions with language models, where users play a crucial role in guiding and shaping the output by framing their queries with clarity and specificity. As users master the art of crafting precise requests, they unlock the full potential of ChatGPT in generating responses tailored to their unique requirements.

Queries: Simple to Complex

The way you phrase your requests can indeed impact the type and quality of responses you receive from ChatGPT.

Here are some samples ranging from simple to more complex requests:

Simple Requests:

In the realm of simple requests, users can employ ChatGPT to elicit straightforward and concise responses. These queries often target specific pieces of information or entertainment. Let's delve into each example and explore additional instances that fall within this category.

1. "Tell me a joke."
   - This request prompts ChatGPT to generate a

humorous statement or a short narrative designed to invoke laughter. For example, "Why did the scarecrow win an award? Because he was outstanding in his field!

Additional Examples:

- "Share a pun related to animals."
- "Provide a lighthearted anecdote about technology."
- "Craft a one-liner about science."

2. "Describe the process of photosynthesis."

- This question prompts ChatGPT to explain the fundamental process by which plants convert sunlight into energy. An example response might be, "Photosynthesis is the biochemical process by which green plants and some bacteria convert sunlight into energy, utilizing carbon dioxide and water to produce glucose and oxygen."

Additional Examples:

- "Explain the water cycle in a few sentences."
- "Describe the stages of mitosis in a cell."

- "Summarize the concept of natural selection."

3. "Summarize the plot of Romeo and Juliet."

- This request involves providing a condensed overview of the iconic Shakespearean tragedy. For instance, "Romeo and Juliet is a tragic love story between two young members of feuding families, the Montagues and Capulets, ultimately ending in the untimely deaths of the titular characters."

Additional Examples:

- "Give a brief summary of 'To Kill a Mockingbird.'"
- "Outline the main events in 'The Great Gatsby.'"
- "Summarize the plot of 'Harry Potter and the Sorcerer's Stone.'"

4. "Explain the concept of gravity."

   - This inquiry aims to receive a concise explanation of the force that attracts objects with mass towards each other. For example, "Gravity is the force that pulls objects towards the center of the Earth, dependent on the masses of the objects and the distance between them."

   Additional Examples:

   - "Elaborate on the concept of inertia."

   - "Define the laws of thermodynamics."

   - "Clarify the principles of relativity proposed by Einstein."

These examples illustrate the simplicity and clarity of queries falling under the category of simple requests. Users seeking quick information or brief entertainment can utilize such prompts to efficiently engage with ChatGPT.

notes

_____
_____
_____
_____
_____
_____
_____
_____
_____
_____
_____
_____
_____
_____
_____
_____
_____
_____
_____
_____
_____
_____
_____

Intermediate Requests:

Intermediate requests involve soliciting more elaborate and developed responses from ChatGPT. These queries often require a more nuanced understanding of a topic or the creation of content with a moderate level of complexity. Let's dive into each example and provide additional instances that align with this level of request.

1. "Write a short paragraph about the benefits of regular exercise."

- This request prompts ChatGPT to provide a more detailed and comprehensive response regarding the advantages of maintaining a regular exercise routine. For instance, "Regular exercise offers a myriad of benefits, including improved cardiovascular health, enhanced mood through the release of endorphins, weight management, and increased muscle strength and flexibility."

- Additional Examples:

- "Elaborate on the psychological benefits of mindfulness meditation."

- "Describe the positive effects of a balanced diet on overall well-being."

- "Explain how adequate sleep contributes to cognitive function."

2. "Compose a poem about the beauty of nature."

- This request invites ChatGPT to create a poetic piece celebrating the wonders of the natural world. An example response might be, "In meadows green and mountains high, nature's beauty fills the sky. A dance of leaves in the gentle breeze, a symphony of life among the trees."

- Additional Examples:

- "Craft a haiku capturing the essence of a sunset."

- "Write a sonnet about the changing seasons."

- "Compose a free-verse poem inspired by the

ocean."

3. "Explain the impact of climate change on biodiversity."

- This inquiry delves into the intricate relationship between climate change and the diversity of life on Earth. For example, "Climate change poses a threat to biodiversity as rising temperatures, altered precipitation patterns, and extreme weather events disrupt ecosystems, leading to habitat loss, shifts in species distribution, and increased risks of extinction."

- Additional Examples:

- "Detail the consequences of deforestation on global biodiversity."
- "Discuss the role of pollution in the decline of marine biodiversity."
- "Examine the impact of invasive species on local ecosystems."

4. "Compare and contrast the main characters

in a novel of your choice."

 - This request involves analyzing and highlighting the similarities and differences between characters in a chosen literary work. For instance, "In George Orwell's '1984,' Winston Smith and Julia share a rebellious spirit against the oppressive regime, but their motivations, backgrounds, and outcomes diverge, showcasing the complexities of individual resistance."

 - Additional Examples:

  - "Compare the character development of Hamlet and Macbeth in Shakespearean tragedies."

  - "Contrast the protagonists in 'Pride and Prejudice' and 'Sense and Sensibility.'"

  - "Examine the themes represented by different characters in a dystopian novel."

These examples demonstrate the intermediate nature of requests that delve deeper into topics, requiring more elaborate and nuanced responses from ChatGPT. Users seeking in-depth insights or more complex creative content can leverage these types of prompts.

notes

_____
_____
_____
_____
_____
_____
_____
_____
_____
_____
_____
_____
_____
_____
_____
_____
_____
_____
_____
_____
_____
_____

Complex Requests:

Complex requests demand a higher level of engagement and creative thinking from ChatGPT. Users can expect more detailed and sophisticated responses that involve intricate scenarios, analyses, or creative constructs. Let's delve into each example and offer additional instances.

1. "Imagine you are a historian writing about the causes and consequences of a fictional war in the 22nd century."
   - This request immerses ChatGPT in a speculative historical context, requiring the generation of intricate details about the causes, course, and aftermath of a war set in the 22nd century. For instance, "In the 22nd century, the war erupted due to disputes over dwindling natural resources, exacerbated by geopolitical tensions and the rise of autonomous weapon systems. The consequences included widespread environmental devastation, the reshaping of global power

dynamics, and the emergence of new alliances."

   - Additional Examples:
   - "Describe the cultural and technological shifts following a successful manned mission to Mars in the 23rd century."
   - "Imagine the political landscape of a united Earth facing an extraterrestrial threat in the 25th century."
   - "Craft a historical account of the development and consequences of a breakthrough in time travel technology."

2. "Craft a persuasive argument for the implementation of sustainable energy policies, addressing both economic and environmental aspects."
   - This request challenges ChatGPT to articulate a compelling case for sustainable energy policies, considering their impact on both the economy and the environment. An example response might be, "Implementing sustainable energy policies not

only mitigates the environmental impact of traditional energy sources but also stimulates economic growth by fostering innovation, creating jobs in the renewable energy sector, and reducing long-term reliance on finite resources."

  - **Additional Examples:**
  - "Argue for the benefits of a universal basic income system, emphasizing its economic and social advantages."
  - "Persuade policymakers to invest in education reform, outlining the long-term economic and societal benefits."
  - "Craft a compelling case for the exploration and colonization of exoplanets, considering both scientific and economic motivations."

3. **"Create a dialogue** between two characters discussing the ethical implications of advanced artificial intelligence."
  - This request involves constructing a conversation between two characters delving into

the ethical dimensions of advanced AI. For instance, "Character A: 'The development of sentient AI raises questions about consciousness and rights.' Character B: 'But what if it leads to unprecedented advancements in medicine and eliminates dangerous tasks for humans?'"

  - Additional Examples:
    - "Write a dialogue between scientists debating the ethical considerations of human genetic engineering."
    - "Craft a conversation between a journalist and a privacy advocate discussing the implications of ubiquitous surveillance technology."
    - "Imagine a debate between two philosophers on the moral aspects of mind-uploading technology."

4. "As a science fiction writer, describe a futuristic cityscape with advanced technology and societal changes."
  - This imaginative request prompts ChatGPT to

create a vivid depiction of a futuristic city, encompassing technological advancements and societal shifts. An example response could be, "In the sprawling metropolis of NeoElysium, towering skyscrapers seamlessly integrate with nature through vertical gardens, while flying vehicles zip through the sky. A society driven by artificial intelligence fosters unprecedented connectivity, but questions of privacy and human autonomy linger."

- **Additional Examples:**
  - "Envision a world where augmented reality has transformed everyday life, and people navigate a digital and physical hybrid existence."
  - "Describe a utopian society where advanced technology has eradicated poverty, and humans live in harmony with nature."
  - "Craft a dystopian cityscape where invasive technologies control every aspect of citizens' lives, exploring the consequences of unchecked technological surveillance."

These examples showcase the intricate and multifaceted nature of complex requests, challenging ChatGPT to provide detailed and thought-provoking content. Users seeking elaborate scenarios, in-depth analyses, or creative constructs can leverage these types of prompts.

notes

Specialized Requests:

Specialized requests require ChatGPT to demonstrate a deep understanding of specific fields, industries, or domains. Users can expect detailed, informed, and expert-level responses. Let's delve into each example and offer additional instances.

1. "Provide a detailed analysis of the economic impact of a hypothetical global pandemic on the technology sector."

   - This request delves into the intricate relationship between a global pandemic and its economic consequences, focusing specifically on the technology sector. An example response might be, "The hypothetical global pandemic, akin to the challenges posed by COVID-19, would likely lead to increased demand for remote collaboration tools, cybersecurity solutions, and healthcare technologies. However, disruptions in the supply chain, reduced consumer spending, and uncertainties could impede growth in hardware manufacturing and certain tech services."

 - **Additional Examples:**
  - "Analyze the effects of regulatory changes on the pharmaceutical industry in the context of a global health crisis."
  - "Examine the cybersecurity vulnerabilities exposed by a large-scale cyberattack on critical infrastructure."
  - "Explore the economic implications of a breakthrough in quantum computing technology on various industries."

2. "Draft a press release announcing the launch of a revolutionary product in the field of renewable energy."
 - This request challenges ChatGPT to create a press release that effectively communicates the launch of a groundbreaking renewable energy product. For instance, "In an unprecedented stride toward sustainability, [Company Name] proudly

unveils the SolarHarmony, a revolutionary solar panel technology that not only boosts energy efficiency by 30% but also incorporates recycled materials, reinforcing our commitment to a greener future."

   - Additional Examples:
   - "Compose a product announcement for an innovative carbon capture technology designed for industrial applications."
   - "Craft a press release introducing a bio-inspired energy storage solution inspired by nature."
   - "Develop a communication strategy for the launch of an eco-friendly transportation system powered by renewable energy."

3. "Develop a lesson plan for teaching advanced calculus to high school students, incorporating real-world applications."
   - This educational request prompts ChatGPT to design a comprehensive lesson plan that engages

high school students by integrating advanced calculus concepts with real-world applications. An example response might be, "Lesson 1: Introduction to Derivatives - Apply derivatives to analyze rates of change in real-world scenarios like population growth or chemical reactions. Lesson 2: Integration and Area Under the Curve - Explore how integral calculus is used to calculate areas and volumes, drawing connections to physics and engineering."

- **Additional Examples:**
  - "Design a curriculum module introducing high school students to machine learning concepts through interactive programming exercises."
  - "Create a lesson plan for teaching the principles of sustainable agriculture in a biology class, incorporating hands-on experiments."
  - "Outline a course module on the applications of statistical analysis in social sciences for high school students."

4. "Compose a speech for a CEO addressing the company's stakeholders about the future direction of the organization."

 - This corporate request involves crafting a speech that articulates the CEO's vision and strategic goals for the organization. For instance, "Ladies and gentlemen, today marks a pivotal moment in our journey. As we navigate the challenges of an ever-evolving market, we commit to fostering innovation, embracing sustainability, and amplifying our global impact. Together, we will spearhead initiatives that redefine our industry and propel us into a future where success is synonymous with positive societal change."

 - Additional Examples:
 - "Write a script for a TED Talk where a tech entrepreneur discusses the ethical responsibilities of AI developers and the future of artificial intelligence."
 - "Draft a town hall speech for a community-focused CEO outlining initiatives for corporate

social responsibility and community engagement."

- "Compose a presentation script for a CEO unveiling a strategic partnership that will reshape the company's position in the market."

These examples highlight the specialized nature of requests that demand a high level of expertise and domain-specific knowledge. Users seeking detailed analyses, professional documents, or expert-level content can leverage these types of prompts.

notes

_____
_____
_____
_____
_____
_____
_____
_____
_____
_____
_____
_____
_____
_____
_____
_____
_____
_____
_____
_____
_____
_____
_____

Interactive Requests:

Interactive requests involve a dynamic exchange where ChatGPT actively collaborates with the user, providing guidance, suggestions, or even participating in role-playing scenarios. These prompts foster creative collaboration and allow users to actively shape the content. Let's delve into each example and offer additional instances.

1. "Role-play as a character from a specific time period or fictional universe and engage in a conversation with me."

 - This request invites ChatGPT to adopt the persona of a character, bringing them to life in a dynamic conversation. For example, "Character A: 'Greetings, traveler! I am Elandria, an elven archer from the mystical land of Eldoria. What brings you to our enchanted realm?' User: 'I seek the guidance of the elves on a quest to save my village from an ancient curse.'"

- Additional Examples:

- "Immerse yourself as a detective from the noir era, engaging in a dialogue with a mysterious client seeking your investigative skills."

- "Role-play as a futuristic AI assistant, assisting a user in navigating a complex virtual reality simulation."

- "Embark on a conversation as a historical figure, such as Leonardo da Vinci, discussing your artistic innovations with a curious admirer."

2. "Help me brainstorm ideas for a science fiction short story involving time travel."

- This collaborative request prompts ChatGPT to contribute creative ideas for a science fiction narrative. An example response might be, "Imagine a protagonist who discovers a time-traveling device in their grandfather's attic. As they explore different eras, they inadvertently alter key historical events, leading to unforeseen consequences. The climax involves a race against time to correct the timeline before irreversible changes occur."

- Additional Examples:

- "Brainstorm a plot where time travel is a consequence of a scientific experiment gone wrong, creating parallel universes."

- "Develop a story where characters from different time periods collaborate to prevent a future catastrophe using time travel."

- "Craft a narrative where time travelers inadvertently encounter their past and future selves, creating a complex web of interactions."

3. "Guide me through creating a compelling narrative for a video game storyline, including key plot points and character development."

- This request involves collaborative world-building and storytelling for a video game. For instance, "Begin with an ordinary protagonist discovering latent magical abilities. As they embark on a quest to master these powers, they uncover a prophecy foretelling an imminent cosmic threat. Along the journey, they recruit diverse companions, each with unique skills and backgrounds, culminating in an epic confrontation against a malevolent cosmic entity."

  - **Additional Examples:**
  - "Create a game narrative set in a cyberpunk city, where the protagonist navigates corporate intrigue and a rebellion against a powerful AI."
  - "Outline a storyline for a fantasy RPG where the player's choices impact not only the narrative but also the game world's political landscape."
  - "Develop a plot for a horror-themed survival game set in an abandoned research facility where experiments have gone awry."

4. "Assist me in drafting an engaging and informative social media post about a recent scientific discovery."
  - This request requires ChatGPT to collaboratively craft a social media post that captures attention and conveys information effectively. An example response might be, "Exciting Breakthrough in Astrophysics!

Researchers have detected signals from a distant galaxy, unraveling mysteries of the cosmos. Dive into the details of this cosmic revelation and join the conversation about our place in the vast universe! #SpaceDiscovery #ScienceRevolution"

- **Additional Examples:**
  - "Compose a tweet highlighting a groundbreaking medical discovery and its potential impact on public health."
  - "Craft an Instagram post celebrating a scientific achievement in renewable energy and encouraging sustainable practices."
  - "Create a Facebook update explaining a breakthrough in AI research and its applications in everyday life."

These examples illustrate the dynamic and collaborative nature of interactive requests, allowing users to actively participate in creative processes, whether through role-play, brainstorming, narrative development, or crafting engaging content. Users seeking collaborative and engaging interactions can leverage these types of prompts.

Remember, the more specific and detailed your request, the better ChatGPT can generate a response tailored to your needs. Feel free to experiment and iterate on your prompts to achieve the desired results!

notes

Advice to New Users from ChatGPT

For new users of ChatGPT, here are some valuable pieces of advice to enhance your experience:

1. Be Clear and Specific:

Crafting clear and specific prompts is essential for maximizing the effectiveness of your interactions with ChatGPT. Clearly state the information or assistance you are seeking, avoiding vague or ambiguous language. For instance, instead of asking, "Tell me about technology," you might specify, "Provide a concise overview of recent advancements in artificial intelligence and their applications in healthcare." This clarity helps ChatGPT grasp the nuances of your request and generate responses that precisely match your needs. Whether you're seeking information, creative content, or problem-solving assistance, the more details you provide, the more accurate and relevant the responses will be.

2. Experiment and Iterate:

Embrace a spirit of experimentation when interacting with ChatGPT. If the initial response doesn't align with your expectations, don't hesitate to experiment with different phrasings and iterate on your prompts. Refine your request by adding or modifying details to guide ChatGPT toward the desired outcome. For example, if you're seeking creative content, try varying the tone or style instructions to explore different creative outputs. This iterative approach allows you to fine-tune your communication with the model, increasing the likelihood of receiving responses that align more closely with your intent.

3. Use System Instructions:

Take advantage of the system instruction feature to influence ChatGPT's behavior. By including specific instructions at the beginning of your input, you can shape the tone, format, or style of the generated response. For instance, if you're seeking a formal and informative answer, you can start your prompt with, "Provide a detailed analysis of..." On the other hand, if you're interested in a creative or casual response, you might instruct, "Imagine a scenario where..." These instructions act as a guiding framework for ChatGPT, helping you receive content that aligns with your preferences. This feature adds a layer of customization to your interactions, making ChatGPT a more versatile tool for your specific needs.

4. Ask in Stages:

When faced with complex questions or multifaceted tasks, it's beneficial to employ a strategy of breaking them down into smaller, more manageable parts. This approach helps both you and ChatGPT by providing a clear structure for the conversation. Instead of posing a broad question like, "Explain the impact of renewable energy on global economies and the environment," consider dividing it into stages. Start by asking, "What are the environmental benefits of renewable energy?" Once you have a response, you can delve deeper with follow-up questions. This method enhances the clarity of your inquiry and facilitates more detailed and focused responses from ChatGPT.

5. Provide Context:

Context is key to obtaining accurate and relevant information or content from ChatGPT. When framing your question or request, offer contextual details about the specific topic, setting, or scenario you are referring to. For example, instead of simply asking, "Tell me about space exploration," you could provide context by specifying, "In the context of space exploration, discuss recent developments in Mars rover missions." By supplying pertinent information, you guide ChatGPT's understanding, ensuring that the generated content aligns more closely with your intended focus. Contextualizing your inquiries enhances the quality and relevance of the responses you receive.

6. Utilize Specialized Prompts:

For queries that delve into specialized or technical domains, it is crucial to be explicit about the subject's domain or field. This specificity enables ChatGPT to provide more accurate and informed responses. For instance, if you're interested in the latest advancements in artificial intelligence, you might phrase your question as, "In the field of artificial intelligence, discuss recent breakthroughs in natural language processing." This precision ensures that ChatGPT draws from relevant knowledge and delivers responses that reflect a deeper understanding of the specified domain. Whether you're seeking scientific insights, industry-specific information, or technical details, employing specialized prompts enhances the accuracy and depth of ChatGPT's responses.

7. Experiment with Creative Prompts:

For users interested in unleashing the creative

potential of ChatGPT, it's highly beneficial to experiment with imaginative prompts. Whether you're into creative writing or storytelling, this is an opportunity to explore the vast realms of fiction. Encourage ChatGPT to conjure up fictional scenarios, invent intriguing characters, or craft captivating dialogues. Instead of asking for straightforward information, prompt the model with requests like, "Create a short story set in a future where humans coexist with sentient robots." By engaging with ChatGPT in this way, users can unlock its ability to generate unique and imaginative content, making the creative process more dynamic and inspiring.

8. Review and Refine:

After receiving responses from ChatGPT, take a moment to review the content. Assess whether it aligns with your expectations and needs. If necessary, don't hesitate to refine your initial request or ask follow-up questions to delve deeper into a topic. For instance, if the response provides valuable insights but lacks a specific detail, refine your request by asking, "Can you elaborate on the implications of this in the context of [specific aspect]?" This reviewing and refining process ensures that your interaction with ChatGPT is a dynamic and iterative exchange, enhancing the quality and relevance of the information or content you seek.

9. Enjoy the Process:
Approaching your interactions with ChatGPT as a collaborative and enjoyable process can significantly enhance your overall experience. Whether you're seeking information, creative content, or assistance with problem-solving, maintaining an engaged and positive mindset fosters a more rewarding interaction. Acknowledge the potential for surprises and creativity, and embrace the conversational aspect of your exchanges with the model. By doing so, you not only optimize the utility of ChatGPT but also turn the interaction into an enjoyable journey

of exploration and discovery. This approach contributes to a more fulfilling and enriching experience, making your use of ChatGPT both productive and engaging.

10. Understand the Model Limitations:

While ChatGPT is a potent tool, it's crucial to be aware of its limitations. Recognize that the model may not always furnish completely accurate or up-to-date information, especially in rapidly evolving fields. Additionally, ChatGPT has a penchant for generating creative content, sometimes fictional in nature. It's important to approach responses with a discerning eye, particularly when seeking factual information. For critical applications, verification from authoritative sources is recommended. Understanding the model's limitations ensures a realistic expectation of its capabilities and aids users in making informed decisions about the information they extract from ChatGPT.

11. Explore Different Genres:

To unlock the full potential of ChatGPT, venture into various genres and purposes. Beyond casual conversation, consider using the tool for information retrieval, creative writing, problem-solving, and more. Experimenting with different types of prompts allows users to appreciate the versatility of ChatGPT. For example, you can transition from asking factual questions to seeking assistance in crafting a poem or generating a fictional dialogue. This exploration broadens the scope of your interactions, showcasing the model's adaptability across diverse scenarios and creative endeavors.

12. Provide Feedback:

User feedback plays a pivotal role in refining and enhancing the capabilities of ChatGPT. If you observe areas where responses could be improved, encounter issues, or have suggestions for enhancements, consider providing feedback. Constructive input aids in the continual development and fine-tuning of the model, ensuring it evolves to better meet user needs. Whether it's about refining specific behaviors, enhancing accuracy in certain domains, or suggesting new features, your feedback contributes to the ongoing improvement of ChatGPT. This collaborative feedback loop fosters a dynamic relationship between users and the model, enhancing the overall utility and effectiveness of the tool over time.

Remember, ChatGPT is a tool designed to assist and collaborate with users. Tailoring your approach and experimenting with different types of prompts will help you make the most out of your interactions. Enjoy the journey of exploring and utilizing ChatGPT's capabilities!

Unlocking Infinite Detail

The Art of Relentless Inquiry

In the enchanting realm of ChatGPT, the journey of exploration is akin to the persistent curiosity of a child armed with an insatiable appetite for understanding the world. To master the art of extracting copious details from this digital oracle, one must adopt the mentality of that ever-curious child, incessantly asking, "But why?" and "How?" until every crevice of knowledge is illuminated.

The Power of Relentless Inquiry:

Imagine the inquisitive child who, upon hearing a simple explanation, doesn't settle but instead probes further, demanding more intricate details. In the realm of ChatGPT, users can harness this power of relentless inquiry to unravel the depths of any subject. The beauty lies in the willingness of ChatGPT to engage in an ongoing dialogue, providing layer upon layer of information with each successive prompt.

But Why? Unraveling the Layers:

Much like the persistent child, users can continually peel back the layers of a topic by appending their prompts with "But why?" This prompts ChatGPT to delve deeper into the rationale, causes, and underlying principles. For instance, if the initial response explains the basics of climate change, a follow-up prompt could be, "But why does the increase in greenhouse gases lead to rising temperatures?"

How? The Mechanics Unveiled:

The relentless pursuit of knowledge involves a keen focus on the mechanics. Users can emulate the child's unyielding curiosity by incorporating "How?" into their prompts. For instance, if ChatGPT provides an overview of artificial intelligence, follow up with, "How do neural networks process information in machine learning?"

When? Unveiling the Chronology:

To construct a comprehensive narrative, users can borrow the child's penchant for understanding timelines. The strategic use of "When?" in prompts prompts ChatGPT to elucidate the chronological aspects of a given topic. For example, if the initial response touches on historical events, a follow-up prompt might be, "When did this particular development significantly impact society?"

Wearing Out the Virtual Inquirer:

In the realm of ChatGPT, there's no risk of wearing out a virtual entity. Instead, users can persistently prompt for more details, exhausting the depths of the model's knowledge. It's a dance of perpetual questioning, each prompt peeling away another layer until the user is satisfied with the richness of information.

Strategies for Maximum Detail Extraction:

1. Layered Prompts: Build your questions in layers, starting with broad inquiries and progressively narrowing down to more specific details.

2. Strategic Follow-Ups: Tailor your follow-up prompts strategically. If an answer introduces a new concept, inquire further about that concept to deepen your understanding.

3. Chronological Exploration: Use time-based prompts to explore the historical evolution of a topic, uncovering crucial milestones and changes over time.

4. Comparative Analysis: Encourage ChatGPT to

provide comparative insights by prompting for contrasts, similarities, and connections between different elements within a subject.

5. Scenario-Based Inquiry: Pose hypothetical scenarios to extract nuanced responses. For instance, "In a scenario where XYZ occurs, what would be the implications on ABC?"

Embrace the spirit of a tireless child seeking to unravel the mysteries of the universe, and with each additional "Why," "How," and "When," witness the depth and richness of knowledge that ChatGPT unfolds. The journey of relentless inquiry promises not just answers but a profound exploration into the intricacies of any subject.

Here is an example of output from ChatGPT first given for 10, 11, and 12 in previous chapter:

10. Understand the Model Limitations:

- Be aware of the model's limitations. While ChatGPT is a powerful tool, it may not always provide accurate or up-to-date information, and it might generate creative but fictional content.

11. Explore Different Genres:

- Try using ChatGPT for various purposes, from casual conversation and information retrieval to creative writing and problem-solving. Exploring different genres helps you understand the versatility of the tool.

12. Provide Feedback:

- If you notice areas where the response could be improved or if you encounter any issues, consider providing feedback. Feedback from users helps in refining and enhancing the capabilities of ChatGPT.

After requesting ChatGPT to expand on each paragraph:

10. Understand the Model Limitations:

While ChatGPT is a potent tool, it's crucial to be aware of its limitations. Recognize that the model may not always furnish completely accurate or up-to-date information, especially in rapidly evolving fields. Additionally, ChatGPT has a penchant for generating creative content, sometimes fictional in nature. It's important to approach responses with a discerning eye, particularly when seeking factual information. For critical applications, verification from authoritative sources is recommended. Understanding the model's limitations ensures a realistic expectation of its capabilities and aids users in making informed decisions about the information they extract from ChatGPT.

11. Explore Different Genres:

To unlock the full potential of ChatGPT, venture into various genres and purposes. Beyond casual conversation, consider using the tool for information retrieval, creative writing, problem-solving, and more. Experimenting with different types of prompts allows users to appreciate the versatility of ChatGPT. For example, you can transition from asking factual questions to seeking assistance in crafting a poem or generating a fictional dialogue. This exploration broadens the scope of your interactions, showcasing the model's adaptability across diverse scenarios and creative endeavors.

12. Provide Feedback:

User feedback plays a pivotal role in refining and enhancing the capabilities of ChatGPT. If you observe areas where responses could be improved, encounter issues, or have suggestions for enhancements, consider providing feedback. Constructive input aids in the continual development and fine-tuning of the model, ensuring it evolves to better meet user needs. Whether it's about refining specific behaviors, enhancing accuracy in certain domains, or suggesting new features, your feedback contributes to the ongoing improvement of ChatGPT. This collaborative feedback loop fosters a dynamic relationship between users and the model, enhancing the overall utility and effectiveness of the tool over time.

MY SENTENCE:

As you can see, by asking to "Expand" on content, you get AI to delve deeper into providing more information.

EXPANDED:

When you specifically request the AI to "Expand" on content, you initiate a process that prompts the model to delve deeper into the given subject, thereby eliciting a more comprehensive and detailed response. In this context, the term "Expand" acts as a directive, signaling to the AI that you desire a more thorough exploration of the topic at hand. This instruction guides the model to go beyond surface-level information and to furnish additional details, nuances, and context related to the initial content. It's a powerful cue that encourages the AI to unfold layers of knowledge, offering a richer and more elaborate understanding of the subject matter. The result is a response that not only builds upon the existing information but also provides a deeper and more nuanced perspective, catering to your quest for a more in-depth exploration.

Summary:

"Unlocking Infinite Detail" delves into the captivating world of ChatGPT, comparing the exploration within it to the unwavering curiosity of a child. The narrative encourages users to embrace the relentless inquiry akin to a child incessantly asking "But why?" and "How?" to unveil the intricacies of any subject.

The power of relentless inquiry is highlighted as users leverage ChatGPT's willingness to engage in ongoing dialogue, peeling back layers of information with each successive prompt. Drawing parallels to a persistent child, the text emphasizes the effectiveness of appending prompts with "But why?" to delve deeper into the rationale, causes, and underlying principles of a topic.

The journey unfolds with users emulating a child's curiosity by incorporating "How?" into prompts, focusing on the mechanics of a subject. The strategic use of "When?" is explored to unveil chronological aspects, constructing a comprehensive narrative. The concept of wearing out a virtual inquirer is debunked, as users are encouraged to persistently prompt for more details, engaging in a dance of perpetual questioning until satisfaction with the richness of information is achieved.

Strategies for maximum detail extraction are outlined, including layered prompts, strategic follow-ups, chronological exploration, comparative analysis, and scenario-based inquiry. Each strategy is presented as a tool for users to extract nuanced responses and deepen their understanding of a subject.

Ultimately, the narrative invites readers to embrace the spirit of a tireless child in their interactions with ChatGPT. Through the art of relentless inquiry, users are promised not just answers but a profound exploration into the intricacies of any subject, unlocking layers of knowledge with each additional "Why," "How," and "When."

Navigating the Spectrum

From Simple Queries to Complex Endeavors

Here are additional examples of simple, intermediate, and complex Chat requests.

Simple Requests:

1. "Tell me a joke."
2. "Define photosynthesis."
3. "Summarize the plot of 'Alice in Wonderland.'"
4. "Explain how a refrigerator works."
5. "List three benefits of regular exercise."
6. "Describe the process of making chocolate."
7. "What is the capital of France?"
8. "Tell me about the history of the internet."
9. "Explain the concept of supply and demand."
10. "Who is Marie Curie?"
11. "What are the basic rules of chess?"
12. "Define the term 'global warming.'"

Intermediate Requests:

1. "Write a short paragraph about the impact of social media on society."

2. "Compose a poem about the changing seasons."

3. "Explain the influence of the Renaissance on art and culture."

4. "Compare and contrast the themes of two Shakespearean sonnets."

5. "Describe the implications of artificial intelligence in healthcare."

6. "Discuss the historical context of the Industrial Revolution."

7. "Provide an analysis of the economic theories of Adam Smith."

8. "Write a brief essay on the importance of biodiversity."

9. "Explore the impact of social media on mental health."

10. "Compare the main characters in two different novels."

11. "Describe the process of evolution and natural selection."

12. "Explain the role of mitochondria in cellular respiration."

Complex Requests:

1. "Imagine you are a historian writing about the causes and consequences of a fictional war in the 22nd century."

2. "Craft a persuasive argument for the implementation of sustainable energy policies, addressing both economic and environmental aspects."

3. "Create a dialogue between two characters discussing the ethical implications of advanced artificial intelligence."

4. "As a science fiction writer, describe a futuristic cityscape with advanced technology and societal changes."

5. "Develop a strategic plan for a company entering a new international market, considering cultural, economic, and political factors."

6. "Imagine you are a political analyst analyzing the potential impact of a global economic

recession on international relations."

7. "Craft a proposal for a comprehensive educational reform, considering the challenges and opportunities in the current system."

8. "Write a research paper discussing the ethical considerations in gene editing technologies."

9. "As a technology consultant, outline a plan for implementing a secure and efficient cloud computing infrastructure for a large corporation."

10. "Imagine you are a philosopher discussing the ethical dilemmas surrounding the use of artificial intelligence in decision-making processes."

11. "Draft a fictional speech for a world leader addressing the global challenges of climate change and proposing innovative solutions."

12. "Create a detailed business plan for a startup in the renewable energy sector, covering funding, market analysis, and sustainability strategies."

For more accurate and tailored results from the AI, ensure your chat request is specific and well-defined.

notes

_____
_____
_____
_____
_____
_____
_____
_____
_____
_____
_____
_____
_____
_____
_____
_____
_____
_____
_____
_____
_____
_____
_____
_____

notes

Dear Valued Reader,

I extend our heartfelt gratitude to each one of you for claiming a copy of "AI Crafting Precision: The Art of Effective Queries in AI Conversations." I appreciate your interest in exploring the intricacies of communication with AI, and trust that this guide will serve as a valuable resource in your journey.

In the world of AI, the ability to communicate effectively is a key to unlocking its full potential. I hope that the insights shared in this book empower you to craft queries that yield accurate, relevant, and nuanced responses from AI systems, enhancing your overall experience.

May your exploration into the realm of AI conversations be marked by curiosity, discovery, and success. As you delve into the art of crafting precise queries, may you find the answers you seek and, in doing so, elevate your AI endeavors to new heights.

Once again, thank you for being a part of my global world of book readers and fans. I wish you success and fulfillment in all your AI interactions.

Best Regards,

Bruce Goldwell

PS: Please be sure to visit Amazon and leave a review for this book. Thanks in advance for your honest and heartfelt review.

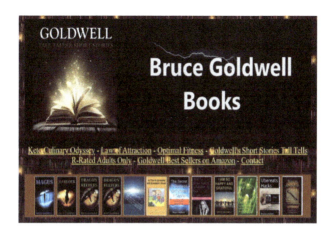

Bruce Goldwell Books

Discover a world of empowerment and transformation with Bruce Goldwell's diverse collection of books. As a prolific author, Goldwell ventures into various genres, offering readers a range of insightful and engaging content.

Self-Help Books: Immerse yourself in Goldwell's self-help books, where he guides readers on a journey of personal development, motivation, and empowerment. These books are crafted to inspire positive change and personal growth.

Fitness Guides: Unlock the secrets to a healthier lifestyle with Goldwell's fitness guides. From workout routines to nutritional advice, his books provide practical insights to help you achieve your fitness goals.

Law of Attraction Books: Delve into the mysteries of the universe with Goldwell's law of attraction books. Explore the principles that govern the law of attraction and learn how to manifest your desires and create the life you envision.

Short Stories: Enjoy a collection of captivating short stories that showcase Goldwell's storytelling prowess. These narratives span genres, offering readers brief escapes into intriguing worlds and thought-provoking scenarios.

Fantasy Adventure Series for Young Readers: Young minds can embark on thrilling adventures with Goldwell's fantasy series. Filled with imagination, magic, and life lessons, these books captivate young readers and ignite their love for storytelling.

Bruce Goldwell's books are a testament to his commitment to helping others lead fulfilling lives. Whether you seek motivation, fitness guidance, or enchanting stories for young readers, Goldwell's literary offerings promise an enriching and transformative reading experience. Explore his collection and embark on a journey of self-discovery and imagination.

About The Author

Bruce Goldwell is a self-help/motivational author and creator of two captivating fantasy adventures, "Dragon Keepers" a six book series and "Starfighters Defending Earth" a three book series. He is an inspiring figure who has overcome significant challenges in his life. As a Vietnam veteran, he experienced homelessness for over ten years.

During these difficult times, Bruce developed a compassionate heart and strong desire to uplift others. While living on the streets, he immersed himself in motivational literature at local bookstores, where he found solace in the works of renowned authors such as the creators of Chicken Soup for the Soul, Bob Proctor, and David Stanley, Elvis Presley's brother.

Inspired by the transformative impact of the film "The Secret," Goldwell penned his first book, "Mastery of Abundant Living: The Keys to Mastering the Law of Attraction." He had the honor of personally presenting the first autographed copy to Bob Proctor. Recognizing that young readers may not typically engage with self-help material, Goldwell brilliantly crafted a fantastical adventure series for teens. Within these enchanting stories, he weaves principles of success and powerful life lessons to ignite hope and encourage personal growth in younger audiences.

Driven by an unwavering belief in the power of his books to change lives, Bruce Goldwell's moving journey from homeless veteran to impactful author has resonated with thousands around the globe. His triumphant quest to help others is a testament to resilience, determination, and the transformative power of words.

Www.mykindlebooks.net